C#.NET AND THE WPF DATAGRID

Working with WMI Async

Richard Thomas
Edwards

CONTENTS

INTRODUCTION

Get ready to learn something new

Wheathter you are a seasoned pro working with the WPF DataGrid or a newbie trying to figure out how to use it, you ether know the WPF DataGrid has a learning curve. And to be perfectly honest, it is not ready for programming it when added to the WPF Application. In-other-words, it is configured wrong when it is automatically added from the toolbox with a double click.

This is the initial XML tag with the default settings:

```
<DataGrid AutoGenerateColumns="False" Height="200"
HorizontalAlignment="Left" Margin="10,10,0,0" Name="dataGrid1"
VerticalAlignment="Top" Width="200" />
```

This is what you see:

To make the DataGrid auto resize:

```
<DataGrid AutoGenerateColumns="False" Height="auto"
HorizontalAlignment="stretch" Name="dataGrid1"
VerticalAlignment="Stretch" Width="auto" />
```

This is the result:

There is one attribute that needs to be discussed. That is AutoGenerateColumns. Currently, it is set to false.

So, I added a couple of columns:

```xml
<DataGrid                AutoGenerateColumns="False"              Height="Auto"
HorizontalAlignment="Stretch"   Name="dataGrid1"   VerticalAlignment="Stretch"
Width="Auto">
    <DataGrid.Columns>
        <DataGridTextColumn Header="ProductID"></DataGridTextColumn>
        <DataGridTextColumn Header="ProductName"></DataGridTextColumn>
    </DataGrid.Columns>
</DataGrid>
```

The grid now looks like this:

What happens if I take something like the DataTable add, the column names and gave it a couple of values?

```
DataTable dt = new DataTable();
dt.Columns.Add("ProductID");
dt.Columns.Add("ProductName");

dt.Rows.Add();
dt.Rows[0][0] = "1";
dt.Rows[0][1] = "Peanut Brittle";


dataGrid1.DataContext = dt;
```

Well that didn't work, did it? Okay so, let's try ItemsSource instead.

```
DataTable dt = new DataTable();
dt.Columns.Add("ProductID");
dt.Columns.Add("ProductName");

dt.Rows.Add();
dt.Rows[0][0] = "1";
dt.Rows[0][1] = "Peanut Brittle";


dataGrid1.ItemsSource = dt.DefaultView;
```

Well now there is something there but not showing.

Back to the DataContext with AutoGenerateColumns set to true:

```
DataTable dt = new DataTable();
dt.Columns.Add("ProductID");
dt.Columns.Add("ProductName");

dt.Rows.Add();
dt.Rows[0][0] = "1";
dt.Rows[0][1] = "Peanut Brittle";


dataGrid1.ItemsSource = dt.DefaultView;
```

ProductID	ProductName	ProductID	ProductName	
		1	Peanut Brittle	

Well that kind of worked. But why two ProductIDs and ProductNames?

As it turns out, when the DataTable was created, it too had its own two Column headers and when added to the runtime code, made sure that the two would show up. The Columns that were physically created and the dynamic columns that were added to create the table.

What about the DataContext? How will that behave?

Okay, nothing happened.

But if I add one Attribute to the DataGrid ItemsSource="{Binding}", it will start working?

ProductID	ProductName	ProductID	ProductName	
		1	Peanut Brittle	

What happens when we also set the binding properties for each column?

```
<DataGrid AutoGenerateColumns="True" Height="Auto"
HorizontalAlignment="Stretch" Name="dataGrid1"
VerticalAlignment="Stretch" Width="Auto" ItemsSource="{Binding}">
        <DataGrid.Columns>
            <DataGridTextColumn Header="ProductID"
Binding="{Binding ProductID}"></DataGridTextColumn>
            <DataGridTextColumn Header="ProductName"
Binding="{Binding ProductName}"></DataGridTextColumn>
        </DataGrid.Columns>
    </DataGrid>
```

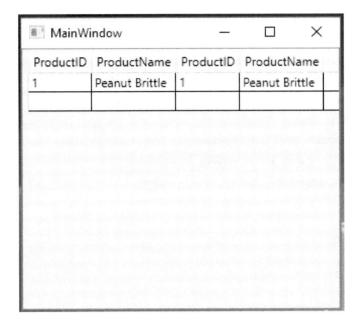

ProductID	ProductName	ProductID	ProductName
1	Peanut Brittle	1	Peanut Brittle

So, if we set the AutoGenerateColumns to false, we get this:

ProductID	ProductName		
1	Peanut Brittle		

So, we've established some rules about how to populate our grid.

The DataGrid's DataContext is the top-level method we can use to populate our DataGrid. Two, while ItemsSource can be set inside code, the physical body of the xml, and also at runtime, - sorry, I didn't mention this before – at this level, it only supports IEnumerable objects. Which means when you use the DataContext, it converts the information into an IEnumerable object which then binds that information to everything else. Three, setting the AutoGenerateColumns attribute to true only works when there are XML tags already written. Otherwise, you get empty duplicates.

MANUALLY POPULATING THE DATAGRID THROUGH CODE

The first thing we're going to do here is to create a solution to a problem almost everyone else never solved.

As with VB.Net and C#.Net – okay, I am sure there are others – there is the concept of a structure. But in C#.Net, the examples show the structure as being used as a type and not as a property that looks something like this:

```
struct Products
{
    public string ProductID;
    public string ProductName;

};
```

The problem is, all you are doing with a structure in C# is making a bunch of names equal to a value type – such as a string – but not creating a named value pair. Put another way, the structure was not based on a property collection but a collection of types – such as a string.

The class, as show below, is doing it right. Meaning the pair of name and value are in property format. So, no matter how you wrote the code for the grid to show both name and value, all you would get is the Name:

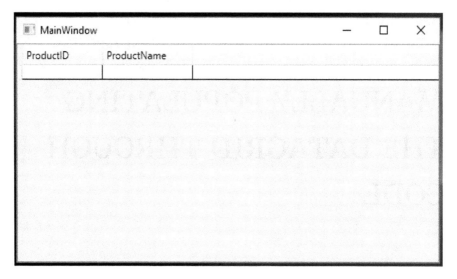

Change the struct to class and add the get\set block to each:

```csharp
class Products
{
    public string ProductID { get; set; }
    public string ProductName { get; set; }

};
```

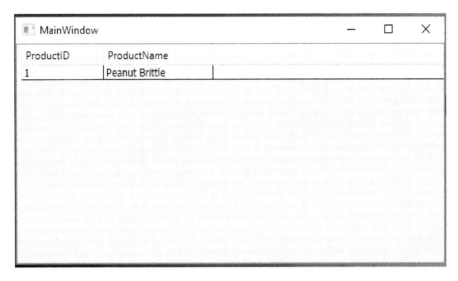

So, why not do the same thing done with the structure as you would with the class?

```
struct Products
{
    public string ProductID { get; set; }
    public string ProductName { get; set; }

};
```

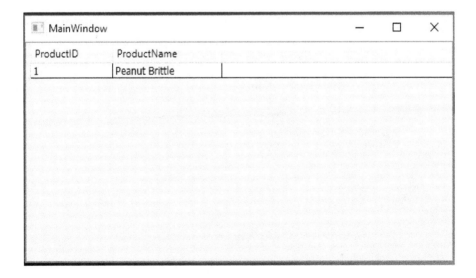

So now, we can take the physical logic:

```
<DataGrid AutoGenerateColumns="False" Height="Auto"
HorizontalAlignment="Stretch" Name="dataGrid1"
VerticalAlignment="Stretch" Width="Auto" ItemsSource="{Binding}">
    <DataGrid.Columns>
        <DataGridTextColumn Header="ProductID"
Binding="{Binding ProductID}" Width="100"
FontFamily="Tahoma"></DataGridTextColumn>
        <DataGridTextColumn Header="ProductName"
Binding="{Binding ProductName}" Width="120"
FontFamily="Tahoma"></DataGridTextColumn>
    </DataGrid.Columns>
</DataGrid>
```

And do it in code:

```
        Binding bi;
        DataGridTextColumn c;

        bi = new Binding("ProductID");
        c = new DataGridTextColumn();
        c.Header = "ProductID";
        c.Binding = bi;
        dataGrid1.Columns.Add(c);

        bi = new Binding("ProductName");
        c = new DataGridTextColumn();
        c.Header = "ProductName";
        c.Binding = bi;
        dataGrid1.Columns.Add(c);

        Products P = new Products();
        P.ProductID = "1";
        P.ProductName = "Peanut Brittle";

        ObservableCollection<Products> list = new
ObservableCollection<Products>();
        list.Add(P);

        this.dataGrid1.ItemsSource = list;
```

The results:

ProductID	ProductName	
1	Peanut Brittle	

MainWindow — □ ×

WELCOME TO WMI IN ASYNC MODE

What do you mean I can't Do that? I just did!

There is nothing more rewarding to me than to be told I can't do something and then prove I can. You can easily add forms to your WPF Application Project by electing to add new items. In order for asynchronous calls to work, you have to have a class that sticks around long enough to receive the information from the event. Forms have that kind of persistence and a loop using DoEvents can be used to stop the form from going out of scope and that is all I need to get my Async code to work.

Below is the core code for all the calls:

```
using System;
using System.Collections.Generic;
using System.ComponentModel;
using System.Data;
using System.Drawing;
using System.Linq;
using System.Text;
using System.Windows.Forms;
using Scripting;
using WbemScripting;

namespace WpfApplication12
{
```

```csharp
    public partial class Form1 : Form
    {
        public Form1()
        {
            InitializeComponent();
        }
        SWbemSink sink = null;

        private void sink_OnCompleted(WbemScripting.WbemErrorEnum
iHResult, WbemScripting.SWbemObject objWbemErrorObject,
WbemScripting.SWbemNamedValueSet objWbemAsyncContext)
        {


        }
        public void sink_OnObjectReady(WbemScripting.SWbemObject
objWbemObject, WbemScripting.SWbemNamedValueSet
objWbemAsyncContext)
        {

        }


        public void Start_Async_Code()
        {

            SWbemLocator l = new SWbemLocator();
            SWbemServices svc = l.ConnectServer("LocalHost",
"root\\cimv2", "", "", "MS_409", "", 128, null);
            svc.Security_.AuthenticationLevel =
WbemAuthenticationLevelEnum.wbemAuthenticationLevelPktPrivacy;
            svc.Security_.ImpersonationLevel =
WbemImpersonationLevelEnum.wbemImpersonationLevelImpersonate;
            sink = new SWbemSink();
            sink.OnCompleted += new
ISWbemSinkEvents_OnCompletedEventHandler(sink_OnCompleted);
            sink.OnObjectReady += new
ISWbemSinkEvents_OnObjectReadyEventHandler(sink_OnObjectReady);
            svc.GetAsync(sink, "Win32_BIOS");


        }
    }
}
```

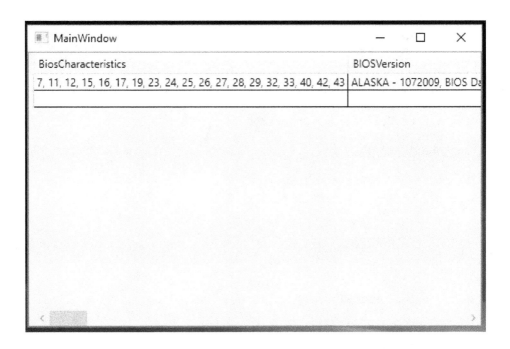

BiosCharacteristics	BIOSVersion
7, 11, 12, 15, 16, 17, 19, 23, 24, 25, 26, 27, 28, 29, 32, 33, 40, 42, 43	ALASKA - 1072009, BIOS Da

I know what you are thinking. All well and good, it works. But how do you get from there to here? Aren't we crossing thread boundaries? There's so many morale and ethical boundaries that...

I got it.

Below is the complete code for Get:

The MainWindow.xaml.cs code:

```csharp
using System;
using System.Collections.Generic;
using System.Linq;
using System.Text;
using System.Windows;
using System.Windows.Controls;
using System.Windows.Data;
using System.Windows.Documents;
using System.Windows.Input;
using System.Windows.Media;
using System.Windows.Media.Imaging;
using System.Windows.Shapes;
using System.Data;
using System.Collections.ObjectModel;
using Scripting;
using WbemScripting;

namespace WpfApplication12
{
    /// <summary>
    /// Interaction logic for Window2.xaml
    /// </summary>
    ///
    public partial class MainWindow : Window
    {
        public MainWindow()
        {
            InitializeComponent();

        }

        Form1 myform = null;

        private void Window_Loaded(object sender, RoutedEventArgs
e)
        {
            myform = new Form1();
            myform.Visible = false;
            myform.Start_Async_Code();


            System.Data.DataTable dt = myform.dt;
```

```
                GridView gv = new GridView();
                Binding bi = null;
                DataGridTextColumn c = null;


                foreach (System.Data.DataColumn column in dt.Columns)
                {

                    bi = new Binding(column.Caption);
                    c = new DataGridTextColumn();
                    c.Header = column.Caption;
                    c.Binding = bi;
                    dataGrid1.Columns.Add(c);
                }

                this.dataGrid1.DataContext = dt;
            }

        }
    }
```

The Form Code:


```
using System;
using System.Collections.Generic;
using System.ComponentModel;
using System.Data;
using System.Drawing;
using System.Linq;
using System.Text;
using System.Windows.Forms;
using Scripting;
using WbemScripting;

namespace WpfApplication12
{
    public partial class Form1 : Form
    {
        public Form1()
        {
            InitializeComponent();
```

```
        }
        SWbemSink sink = null;
        public System.Data.DataTable dt = new
System.Data.DataTable();
        int v = 0;
        int w = 0;
        private void sink_OnCompleted(WbemScripting.WbemErrorEnum
iHResult, WbemScripting.SWbemObject objWbemErrorObject,
WbemScripting.SWbemNamedValueSet objWbemAsyncContext)
        {


        }
        public void sink_OnObjectReady(WbemScripting.SWbemObject
objWbemObject, WbemScripting.SWbemNamedValueSet
objWbemAsyncContext)
        {
            SWbemObjectSet objs = objWbemObject.Instances_(0,
null);
            if (v == 0)
            {
                SWbemObject obj = objs.ItemIndex(0);
                foreach (SWbemProperty prop in obj.Properties_)
                {
                    dt.Columns.Add(prop.Name);
                }
                v=1;
            }
            foreach (SWbemObject obj in objs)
            {
                System.Data.DataRow dr = dt.NewRow();
                foreach (SWbemProperty prop in obj.Properties_)
                {
                    dr[prop.Name] = GetManagementValue(prop.Name,
obj);
                }
                dt.Rows.Add(dr);
            }
            w = 1;
        }
        public void Start_Async_Code()
        {

            SWbemLocator l = new SWbemLocator();
```

```csharp
            SWbemServices svc = l.ConnectServer("LocalHost",
"root\\cimv2", "", "", "MS_409", "", 128, null);
            svc.Security_.AuthenticationLevel =
WbemAuthenticationLevelEnum.wbemAuthenticationLevelPktPrivacy;
            svc.Security_.ImpersonationLevel =
WbemImpersonationLevelEnum.wbemImpersonationLevelImpersonate;
            sink = new SWbemSink();
            sink.OnCompleted += new
ISWbemSinkEvents_OnCompletedEventHandler(sink_OnCompleted);
            sink.OnObjectReady += new
ISWbemSinkEvents_OnObjectReadyEventHandler(sink_OnObjectReady);
            svc.GetAsync(sink, "Win32_BIOS");

            while (w == 0)
            {
                System.Windows.Forms.Application.DoEvents();
            }

        }
        private System.String GetManagementValue(System.String
Name, SWbemObject mo)
        {
            int pos = 0;
            System.String tName = Name + " = ";
            System.String tempstr = mo.GetObjectText_(0);
            pos = tempstr.IndexOf(tName);
            if (pos > -1)
            {
                pos = pos + tName.Length;
                tempstr = tempstr.Substring(pos, tempstr.Length -
pos);

                pos = tempstr.IndexOf(";");
                tempstr = tempstr.Substring(0, pos);
                tempstr = tempstr.Replace("\"", "");
                tempstr = tempstr.Replace("{", "");
                tempstr = tempstr.Replace("}", "");
                if (tempstr.Length > 14)
                {
                    if (mo.Properties_.Item(Name).CIMType ==
WbemCimtypeEnum.wbemCimtypeDatetime)
                    {
                        return tempstr.Substring(5, 2) + "/" +
tempstr.Substring(7, 2) + "/" + tempstr.Substring(0, 4) + " " +
tempstr.Substring(9, 2) + ":" + tempstr.Substring(11, 2) + ":" +
tempstr.Substring(13, 2);
```

```
                }
            }
            return tempstr;
        }
        else
        {
            return "";
        }
    }

    }
}
```

EXECQUERYASYNC AND INSTANCESOFASYNC

Unlike Get, ExecQueryAsync and InstancesOfAsync work the same way The collection of rows or object is sent to the Sink_onObjectReady one at a time. When all of Them have been enumerated through, the Sink_onCompleted gets called. So that's where we tell the loop that v is no longer o and to stop running the loop.

Below is the MainWindow.xaml.cs code:

```
using System;
using System.Collections.Generic;
using System.Linq;
using System.Text;
using System.Windows;
using System.Windows.Controls;
using System.Windows.Data;
using System.Windows.Documents;
using System.Windows.Input;
using System.Windows.Media;
using System.Windows.Media.Imaging;
using System.Windows.Shapes;
using System.Data;
using System.Collections.ObjectModel;
using Scripting;
using WbemScripting;

namespace WpfApplication12
{
    /// <summary>
    /// Interaction logic for Window2.xaml
```

```csharp
        /// </summary>
        ///
        public partial class MainWindow : Window
        {
            public MainWindow()
            {
                InitializeComponent();

            }

            Form2 myform = null;
            private System.String GetManagementValue(System.String
Name, SWbemObject mo)
            {
                int pos = 0;
                System.String tName = Name + " = ";
                System.String tempstr = mo.GetObjectText_(0);
                pos = tempstr.IndexOf(tName);
                if (pos > -1)
                {
                    pos = pos + tName.Length;
                    tempstr = tempstr.Substring(pos, tempstr.Length -
pos);
                    pos = tempstr.IndexOf(";");
                    tempstr = tempstr.Substring(0, pos);
                    tempstr = tempstr.Replace("\"", "");
                    tempstr = tempstr.Replace("{", "");
                    tempstr = tempstr.Replace("}", "");
                    if (tempstr.Length > 14)
                    {
                        if (mo.Properties_.Item(Name).CIMType ==
WbemCimtypeEnum.wbemCimtypeDatetime)
                        {
                            return tempstr.Substring(5, 2) + "/" +
tempstr.Substring(7, 2) + "/" + tempstr.Substring(0, 4) + " " +
tempstr.Substring(9, 2) + ":" + tempstr.Substring(11, 2) + ":" +
tempstr.Substring(13, 2);
                        }
                    }
                    return tempstr;
                }
                else
                {
                    return "";
                }
```

```
        }

        private void Window_Loaded(object sender, RoutedEventArgs
e)
        {
            myform = new Form2();
            myform.Visible = false;
            myform.Start_Async_Code();

            System.Data.DataTable dt = myform.dt;
            GridView gv = new GridView();
            Binding bi = null;
            DataGridTextColumn c = null;


            foreach (System.Data.DataColumn column in dt.Columns)
            {

                bi = new Binding(column.Caption);
                c = new DataGridTextColumn();
                c.Header = column.Caption;
                c.Binding = bi;
                dataGrid1.Columns.Add(c);
            }

            this.dataGrid1.DataContext = dt;
        }

    }
}
```

Here's the form code:

```
using System;
using System.Collections.Generic;
using System.ComponentModel;
using System.Data;
using System.Drawing;
using System.Linq;
using System.Text;
using System.Windows.Forms;
```

```csharp
using Scripting;
using WbemScripting;

namespace WpfApplication12
{
    public partial class Form2 : Form
    {
        public Form2()
        {
            InitializeComponent();
        }
        SWbemSink sink = null;
        public System.Data.DataTable dt = new
System.Data.DataTable();
        int v = 0;
        int w = 0;
        private void sink_OnCompleted(WbemScripting.WbemErrorEnum
iHResult, WbemScripting.SWbemObject objWbemErrorObject,
WbemScripting.SWbemNamedValueSet objWbemAsyncContext)
        {
            w = 1;
        }
        public void sink_OnObjectReady(WbemScripting.SWbemObject
objWbemObject, WbemScripting.SWbemNamedValueSet
objWbemAsyncContext)
        {

            if (v == 0)
            {
                foreach (SWbemProperty prop in
objWbemObject.Properties_)
                {
                    dt.Columns.Add(prop.Name);
                }
                v = 1;
            }
            System.Data.DataRow dr = dt.NewRow();
            foreach (SWbemProperty prop in
objWbemObject.Properties_)
            {
                dr[prop.Name] = GetManagementValue(prop.Name,
objWbemObject);
            }
            dt.Rows.Add(dr);
```

```
        }
        public void Start_Async_Code()
        {

            SWbemLocator l = new SWbemLocator();
            SWbemServices svc = l.ConnectServer("LocalHost",
"root\\cimv2", "", "", "MS_409", "", 128, null);
            svc.Security_.AuthenticationLevel =
WbemAuthenticationLevelEnum.wbemAuthenticationLevelPktPrivacy;
            svc.Security_.ImpersonationLevel =
WbemImpersonationLevelEnum.wbemImpersonationLevelImpersonate;
            sink = new SWbemSink();
            sink.OnCompleted += new
ISWbemSinkEvents_OnCompletedEventHandler(sink_OnCompleted);
            sink.OnObjectReady += new
ISWbemSinkEvents_OnObjectReadyEventHandler(sink_OnObjectReady);
            svc.InstancesOfAsync(sink, "Win32_Process");

            while (w == 0)
            {
                System.Windows.Forms.Application.DoEvents();
            }

        }
        private System.String GetManagementValue(System.String
Name, SWbemObject mo)
        {
            int pos = 0;
            System.String tName = Name + " = ";
            System.String tempstr = mo.GetObjectText_(0);
            pos = tempstr.IndexOf(tName);
            if (pos > -1)
            {
                pos = pos + tName.Length;
                tempstr = tempstr.Substring(pos, tempstr.Length -
pos);
                pos = tempstr.IndexOf(";");
                tempstr = tempstr.Substring(0, pos);
                tempstr = tempstr.Replace("\"", "");
                tempstr = tempstr.Replace("{", "");
                tempstr = tempstr.Replace("}", "");
                if (tempstr.Length > 14)
                {
                    if (mo.Properties_.Item(Name).CIMType ==
WbemCimtypeEnum.wbemCimtypeDatetime)
```

```
            {
                return tempstr.Substring(5, 2) + "/" +
tempstr.Substring(7, 2) + "/" + tempstr.Substring(0, 4) + " " +
tempstr.Substring(9, 2) + ":" + tempstr.Substring(11, 2) + ":" +
tempstr.Substring(13, 2);
            }
        }
        return tempstr;
    }
    else
    {
        return "";
    }
}


}
}
```

Here's an image of the results:

MainWindow	— □ ✕

Caption	CommandLine
System Idle Process	
System	
smss.exe	
csrss.exe	
csrss.exe	
wininit.exe	
winlogon.exe	winlogon.exe
services.exe	
lsass.exe	C:\\Windows\\system32\\lsass.exe
svchost.exe	C:\\Windows\\system32\\svchost.exe -k DcomLaunch
svchost.exe	C:\\Windows\\system32\\svchost.exe -k RPCSS
dwm.exe	\dwm.exe\
svchost.exe	C:\\Windows\\System32\\svchost.exe -k termsvcs
svchost.exe	C:\\Windows\\System32\\svchost.exe -k LocalSystemNetworkRestricted
svchost.exe	C:\\Windows\\System32\\svchost.exe -k LocalServiceNetworkRestricted
svchost.exe	C:\\Windows\\system32\\svchost.exe -k LocalServiceNoNetwork
NVDisplay.Container.exe	\C:\\Program Files\\NVIDIA Corporation\\Display.NvContainer\\NVDisplay.Container
svchost.exe	C:\\Windows\\system32\\svchost.exe -k LocalService
WUDFHost.exe	\C:\\Windows\\System32\\WUDFHost.exe\ -HostGUID:193a1820-d9ac-4997-8c55-b
svchost.exe	C:\\Windows\\System32\\svchost.exe -k NetworkService
svchost.exe	C:\\Windows\\System32\\svchost.exe -k netsvcs
svchost.exe	C:\\Windows\\system32\\svchost.exe -k LocalServiceNetworkRestricted
svchost.exe	C:\\Windows\\System32\\svchost.exe -k WlansvcGroup
svchost.exe	C:\\Windows\\System32\\svchost.exe -k LocalServiceNetworkRestricted
spoolsv.exe	C:\\Windows\\System32\\spoolsv.exe
svchost.exe	C:\\Windows\\system32\\svchost.exe -k apphost
svchost.exe	C:\\Windows\\System32\\svchost.exe -k utcsvc

THE EXECQUERY CODE

Below is the code for the ExecQuery:

The MainWindow.xaml.cs code:

```
using System;
using System.Collections.Generic;
using System.Linq;
using System.Text;
using System.Windows;
using System.Windows.Controls;
using System.Windows.Data;
using System.Windows.Documents;
using System.Windows.Input;
using System.Windows.Media;
using System.Windows.Media.Imaging;
using System.Windows.Shapes;
using System.Data;
using System.Collections.ObjectModel;
using Scripting;
using WbemScripting;

namespace WpfApplication12
{
    /// <summary>
    /// Interaction logic for Window2.xaml
    /// </summary>
    ///
    public partial class MainWindow : Window
    {
        public MainWindow()
        {
            InitializeComponent();

        }
```

```
        Form3 myform = null;

        private void Window_Loaded(object sender, RoutedEventArgs
e)
        {
            myform = new Form3();
            myform.Visible = false;
            myform.Start_Async_Code();


            System.Data.DataTable dt = myform.dt;
            GridView gv = new GridView();
            Binding bi = null;
            DataGridTextColumn c = null;


            foreach (System.Data.DataColumn column in dt.Columns)
            {

                bi = new Binding(column.Caption);
                c = new DataGridTextColumn();
                c.Header = column.Caption;
                c.Binding = bi;
                dataGrid1.Columns.Add(c);
            }

            this.dataGrid1.DataContext = dt;
        }

    }
}
```

The form code:

```
using System;
using System.Collections.Generic;
using System.ComponentModel;
using System.Data;
using System.Drawing;
using System.Linq;
using System.Text;
```

```csharp
using System.Windows.Forms;
using Scripting;
using WbemScripting;

namespace WpfApplication12
{
    public partial class Form3 : Form
    {
        public Form3()
        {
            InitializeComponent();
        }
        SWbemSink sink = null;
        public System.Data.DataTable dt = new
System.Data.DataTable();
        int v = 0;
        int w = 0;
        private void sink_OnCompleted(WbemScripting.WbemErrorEnum
iHResult, WbemScripting.SWbemObject objWbemErrorObject,
WbemScripting.SWbemNamedValueSet objWbemAsyncContext)
        {
            w = 1;
        }
        public void sink_OnObjectReady(WbemScripting.SWbemObject
objWbemObject, WbemScripting.SWbemNamedValueSet
objWbemAsyncContext)
        {

            if (v == 0)
            {
                foreach (SWbemProperty prop in
objWbemObject.Properties_)
                {
                    dt.Columns.Add(prop.Name);
                }
                v = 1;
            }
            System.Data.DataRow dr = dt.NewRow();
            foreach (SWbemProperty prop in
objWbemObject.Properties_)
            {
                dr[prop.Name] = GetManagementValue(prop.Name,
objWbemObject);
            }
            dt.Rows.Add(dr);
```

```
        }
        public void Start_Async_Code()
        {

            SWbemLocator l = new SWbemLocator();
            SWbemServices svc = l.ConnectServer("LocalHost",
"root\\cimv2", "", "", "MS_409", "", 128, null);
            svc.Security_.AuthenticationLevel =
WbemAuthenticationLevelEnum.wbemAuthenticationLevelPktPrivacy;
            svc.Security_.ImpersonationLevel =
WbemImpersonationLevelEnum.wbemImpersonationLevelImpersonate;
            sink = new SWbemSink();
            sink.OnCompleted += new
ISWbemSinkEvents_OnCompletedEventHandler(sink_OnCompleted);
            sink.OnObjectReady += new
ISWbemSinkEvents_OnObjectReadyEventHandler(sink_OnObjectReady);
            svc.ExecQueryAsync(sink, "Select Caption,
ExecutablePath, Description, ProcessID From Win32_Process");

            while (w == 0)
            {
                System.Windows.Forms.Application.DoEvents();
            }

        }
        private System.String GetManagementValue(System.String
Name, SWbemObject mo)
        {
            int pos = 0;
            System.String tName = Name + " = ";
            System.String tempstr = mo.GetObjectText_(0);
            pos = tempstr.IndexOf(tName);
            if (pos > -1)
            {
                pos = pos + tName.Length;
                tempstr = tempstr.Substring(pos, tempstr.Length -
pos);

                pos = tempstr.IndexOf(";");
                tempstr = tempstr.Substring(0, pos);
                tempstr = tempstr.Replace("\"", "");
                tempstr = tempstr.Replace("{", "");
                tempstr = tempstr.Replace("}", "");
                if (tempstr.Length > 14)
                {
```

```csharp
                if (mo.Properties_.Item(Name).CIMType ==
WbemCimtypeEnum.wbemCimtypeDatetime)
                {
                    return tempstr.Substring(5, 2) + "/" +
tempstr.Substring(7, 2) + "/" + tempstr.Substring(0, 4) + " " +
tempstr.Substring(9, 2) + ":" + tempstr.Substring(11, 2) + ":" +
tempstr.Substring(13, 2);
                }
            }
            return tempstr;
        }
        else
        {
            return "";
        }
    }

    }
}
```

THE EXECNOTIFICATIONQUERY ASYNC

Where you decide when to stop

This is the only one where you have to decide how many events you want to trap. If you don't, it will just keep on going and you will never see the results show up in the ListView. Also, there are some distinctive differences in what each of the popular instance event types do that we need to cover before you see the code.

The ___InstanceCreationEvent only gets fired when a process is created.

The ___InstanceDeletionEvent only gets fired when a process is deleted.

The ___InstanceModificationEvent only gets fired when any event happens to a process.

The ___InstanceOperationEvent only gets fired when any of the events above gets fired. Meaning, you must filter for the events you want to add to your DataTable.

Below is the MainWindow.xaml.cs code:

```csharp
using System;
using System.Collections.Generic;
using System.Linq;
using System.Text;
using System.Windows;
using System.Windows.Controls;
using System.Windows.Data;
using System.Windows.Documents;
using System.Windows.Input;
using System.Windows.Media;
using System.Windows.Media.Imaging;
using System.Windows.Shapes;
using System.Data;
using System.Collections.ObjectModel;
using Scripting;
using WbemScripting;

namespace WpfApplication12
{
    /// <summary>
    /// Interaction logic for Window2.xaml
    /// </summary>
    ///
    public partial class MainWindow : Window
    {
        public MainWindow()
        {
            InitializeComponent();

        }

        Form4 myform = null;
        private void Window_Loaded(object sender, RoutedEventArgs e)
        {
            myform = new Form4();
            myform.Visible = false;
            myform.Start_Async_Code();
```

```
            System.Data.DataTable dt = myform.dt;
            GridView gv = new GridView();
            Binding bi = null;
            DataGridTextColumn c = null;


            foreach (System.Data.DataColumn column in dt.Columns)
            {

                bi = new Binding(column.Caption);
                c = new DataGridTextColumn();
                c.Header = column.Caption;
                c.Binding = bi;
                dataGrid1.Columns.Add(c);
            }

            this.dataGrid1.DataContext = dt;
        }

    }
}
```

Here's the form's code For ___InstanceCreationEvent:

```
using System;
using System.Collections.Generic;
using System.ComponentModel;
using System.Data;
using System.Drawing;
using System.Linq;
using System.Text;
using System.Windows.Forms;
using Scripting;
using WbemScripting;

namespace WpfApplication12
{
    public partial class Form4 : Form
    {
        public Form4()
```

```csharp
        {
            InitializeComponent();
        }
        SWbemSink sink = null;
        public System.Data.DataTable dt = new
System.Data.DataTable();
        int v = 0;
        int w = 0;
        private void sink_OnCompleted(WbemScripting.WbemErrorEnum
iHResult, WbemScripting.SWbemObject objWbemErrorObject,
WbemScripting.SWbemNamedValueSet objWbemAsyncContext)
        {
            w = 1;
        }
        public void sink_OnObjectReady(WbemScripting.SWbemObject
objWbemObject, WbemScripting.SWbemNamedValueSet
objWbemAsyncContext)
        {

            SWbemObject obj =
objWbemObject.Properties_.Item("TargetInstance").get_Value();

            if (v == 0)
            {
                foreach (SWbemProperty prop in obj.Properties_)
                {
                    dt.Columns.Add(prop.Name);
                }
                v = 1;
            }
            System.Data.DataRow dr = dt.NewRow();
            foreach (SWbemProperty prop in obj.Properties_)
            {
                dr[prop.Name] = GetManagementValue(prop.Name,
obj);
            }
            dt.Rows.Add(dr);

            v = v + 1;
            if(v == 6)
            {
                sink.Cancel();
            }
```

```csharp
    }

    public void Start_Async_Code()
    {

            SWbemLocator l = new SWbemLocator();
            SWbemServices svc = l.ConnectServer("LocalHost",
"root\\cimv2", "", "", "MS_409", "", 128, null);
            svc.Security_.AuthenticationLevel =
WbemAuthenticationLevelEnum.wbemAuthenticationLevelPktPrivacy;
            svc.Security_.ImpersonationLevel =
WbemImpersonationLevelEnum.wbemImpersonationLevelImpersonate;
            sink = new SWbemSink();
            sink.OnCompleted += new
ISWbemSinkEvents_OnCompletedEventHandler(sink_OnCompleted);
            sink.OnObjectReady += new
ISWbemSinkEvents_OnObjectReadyEventHandler(sink_OnObjectReady);

            svc.ExecNotificationQueryAsync(sink, "Select * From
__InstanceCreationEvent within 1 where TargetInstance ISA
'Win32_Process'");
            while (w == 0)
            {
                System.Windows.Forms.Application.DoEvents();
            }

    }
    private System.String GetManagementValue(System.String
Name, SWbemObject mo)
    {
            int pos = 0;
            System.String tName = Name + " = ";
            System.String tempstr = mo.GetObjectText_(0);
            pos = tempstr.IndexOf(tName);
            if (pos > -1)
            {
                pos = pos + tName.Length;
                tempstr = tempstr.Substring(pos, tempstr.Length -
pos);

                pos = tempstr.IndexOf(";");
                tempstr = tempstr.Substring(0, pos);
                tempstr = tempstr.Replace("\"", "");
                tempstr = tempstr.Replace("{", "");
                tempstr = tempstr.Replace("}", "");
```

```
            if (tempstr.Length > 14)
            {
                if (mo.Properties_.Item(Name).CIMType ==
WbemCimtypeEnum.wbemCimtypeDatetime)
                {
                    return tempstr.Substring(5, 2) + "/" +
tempstr.Substring(7, 2) + "/" + tempstr.Substring(0, 4) + " " +
tempstr.Substring(9, 2) + ":" + tempstr.Substring(11, 2) + ":" +
tempstr.Substring(13, 2);
                }
            }
            return tempstr;
        }
        else
        {
            return "";
        }
    }

}
```

Here's the results:

Caption	CommandLine	CreationClassName	CreationDate
win32calc.exe	\C:\\Windows\\System32\\win32calc.exe\	Win32_Process	08/26/2018 08:24:48
svchost.exe		Win32_Process	08/26/2018 08:24:48
notepad.exe	\C:\\Windows\\system32\\Notepad.exe\	Win32_Process	08/26/2018 08:24:54
wordpad.exe	\C:\\Program Files\\Windows NT\\Accessories\\WORDPAD.EXE\	Win32_Process	08/26/2018 08:25:03
mspaint.exe	\C:\\Windows\\system32\\mspaint.exe\	Win32_Process	08/26/2018 08:25:35
mspaint.exe	\C:\\Windows\\system32\\MSPaint.exe\	Win32_Process	08/26/2018 08:26:02

MainWindow — □ ×

Code For ___InstanceDeletionEvent:

```
using System;
using System.Collections.Generic;
using System.ComponentModel;
using System.Data;
using System.Drawing;
using System.Linq;
using System.Text;
using System.Windows.Forms;
using Scripting;
using WbemScripting;

namespace WpfApplication12
{
    public partial class Form4 : Form
    {
        public Form4()
        {
            InitializeComponent();
        }
        SWbemSink sink = null;
        public System.Data.DataTable dt = new
System.Data.DataTable();
        int v = 0;
        int w = 0;
        private void sink_OnCompleted(WbemScripting.WbemErrorEnum
iHResult, WbemScripting.SWbemObject objWbemErrorObject,
WbemScripting.SWbemNamedValueSet objWbemAsyncContext)
        {
            w = 1;
        }
        public void sink_OnObjectReady(WbemScripting.SWbemObject
objWbemObject, WbemScripting.SWbemNamedValueSet
objWbemAsyncContext)
        {

            SWbemObject obj =
objWbemObject.Properties_.Item("TargetInstance").get_Value();

            if (v == 0)
            {
```

```
                foreach (SWbemProperty prop in obj.Properties_)
                {
                    dt.Columns.Add(prop.Name);
                }
                v = 1;
            }
            System.Data.DataRow dr = dt.NewRow();
            foreach (SWbemProperty prop in obj.Properties_)
            {
                dr[prop.Name] = GetManagementValue(prop.Name,
obj);
            }
            dt.Rows.Add(dr);

            v = v + 1;
            if(v == 6)
            {
                sink.Cancel();
            }



        }

    public void Start_Async_Code()
    {

            SWbemLocator l = new SWbemLocator();
            SWbemServices svc = l.ConnectServer("LocalHost",
"root\\cimv2", "", "", "MS_409", "", 128, null);
            svc.Security_.AuthenticationLevel =
WbemAuthenticationLevelEnum.wbemAuthenticationLevelPktPrivacy;
            svc.Security_.ImpersonationLevel =
WbemImpersonationLevelEnum.wbemImpersonationLevelImpersonate;
            sink = new SWbemSink();
            sink.OnCompleted += new
ISWbemSinkEvents_OnCompletedEventHandler(sink_OnCompleted);
            sink.OnObjectReady += new
ISWbemSinkEvents_OnObjectReadyEventHandler(sink_OnObjectReady);

            svc.ExecNotificationQueryAsync(sink, "Select * From
__InstanceDeletionEvent within 1 where TargetInstance ISA
'Win32_Process'");
            while (w == 0)
            {
```

```csharp
                    System.Windows.Forms.Application.DoEvents();
            }

        }
        private System.String GetManagementValue(System.String
Name, SWbemObject mo)
        {
            int pos = 0;
            System.String tName = Name + " = ";
            System.String tempstr = mo.GetObjectText_(0);
            pos = tempstr.IndexOf(tName);
            if (pos > -1)
            {
                pos = pos + tName.Length;
                tempstr = tempstr.Substring(pos, tempstr.Length -
pos);
                pos = tempstr.IndexOf(";");
                tempstr = tempstr.Substring(0, pos);
                tempstr = tempstr.Replace("\"", "");
                tempstr = tempstr.Replace("{", "");
                tempstr = tempstr.Replace("}", "");
                if (tempstr.Length > 14)
                {
                    if (mo.Properties_.Item(Name).CIMType ==
WbemCimtypeEnum.wbemCimtypeDatetime)
                    {
                        return tempstr.Substring(5, 2) + "/" +
tempstr.Substring(7, 2) + "/" + tempstr.Substring(0, 4) + " " +
tempstr.Substring(9, 2) + ":" + tempstr.Substring(11, 2) + ":" +
tempstr.Substring(13, 2);
                    }
                }
                return tempstr;
            }
            else
            {
                return "";
            }
        }

    }
}
```

The results:

Caption	CommandLine	CreationClassName	CreationDate
win32calc.exe	\C:\\Windows\\System32\\win32calc.exe\	Win32_Process	08/26/2018 08:24:48
svchost.exe		Win32_Process	08/26/2018 08:24:48
notepad.exe	\C:\\Windows\\system32\\Notepad.exe\	Win32_Process	08/26/2018 08:24:54
wordpad.exe	\C:\\Program Files\\Windows NT\\Accessories\\WORDPAD.EXE\	Win32_Process	08/26/2018 08:25:03
mspaint.exe	\C:\\Windows\\system32\\mspaint.exe\	Win32_Process	08/26/2018 08:25:35
mspaint.exe	\C:\\Windows\\system32\\MSPaint.exe\	Win32_Process	08/26/2018 08:26:02

Code For ___InstanceModificationEvent:

```
using System;
using System.Collections.Generic;
using System.ComponentModel;
using System.Data;
using System.Drawing;
using System.Linq;
using System.Text;
using System.Windows.Forms;
using Scripting;
using WbemScripting;

namespace WpfApplication12
{
    public partial class Form4 : Form
    {
        public Form4()
        {
            InitializeComponent();
        }
        SWbemSink sink = null;
        public System.Data.DataTable dt = new
System.Data.DataTable();
```

```
    int v = 0;
    int w = 0;
    private void sink_OnCompleted(WbemScripting.WbemErrorEnum
iHResult, WbemScripting.SWbemObject objWbemErrorObject,
WbemScripting.SWbemNamedValueSet objWbemAsyncContext)
    {
        w = 1;
    }
    public void sink_OnObjectReady(WbemScripting.SWbemObject
objWbemObject, WbemScripting.SWbemNamedValueSet
objWbemAsyncContext)
    {

        SWbemObject obj =
objWbemObject.Properties_.Item("TargetInstance").get_Value();

        if (v == 0)
        {
            foreach (SWbemProperty prop in obj.Properties_)
            {
                dt.Columns.Add(prop.Name);
            }
            v = 1;
        }
        System.Data.DataRow dr = dt.NewRow();
        foreach (SWbemProperty prop in obj.Properties_)
        {
            dr[prop.Name] = GetManagementValue(prop.Name,
obj);
        }
        dt.Rows.Add(dr);

        v = v + 1;
        if(v == 30)
        {
            sink.Cancel();
        }


    }

    public void Start_Async_Code()
    {
```

```csharp
            SWbemLocator l = new SWbemLocator();
            SWbemServices svc = l.ConnectServer("LocalHost",
"root\\cimv2", "", "", "MS_409", "", 128, null);
            svc.Security_.AuthenticationLevel =
WbemAuthenticationLevelEnum.wbemAuthenticationLevelPktPrivacy;
            svc.Security_.ImpersonationLevel =
WbemImpersonationLevelEnum.wbemImpersonationLevelImpersonate;
            sink = new SWbemSink();
            sink.OnCompleted += new
ISWbemSinkEvents_OnCompletedEventHandler(sink_OnCompleted);
            sink.OnObjectReady += new
ISWbemSinkEvents_OnObjectReadyEventHandler(sink_OnObjectReady);

            svc.ExecNotificationQueryAsync(sink, "Select * From
__InstanceModificationEvent within 1 where TargetInstance ISA
'Win32_Process'");
            while (w == 0)
            {
                System.Windows.Forms.Application.DoEvents();
            }


        }
        private System.String GetManagementValue(System.String
Name, SWbemObject mo)
        {
            int pos = 0;
            System.String tName = Name + " = ";
            System.String tempstr = mo.GetObjectText_(0);
            pos = tempstr.IndexOf(tName);
            if (pos > -1)
            {
                pos = pos + tName.Length;
                tempstr = tempstr.Substring(pos, tempstr.Length -
pos);
                pos = tempstr.IndexOf(";");
                tempstr = tempstr.Substring(0, pos);
                tempstr = tempstr.Replace("\"", "");
                tempstr = tempstr.Replace("{", "");
                tempstr = tempstr.Replace("}", "");
                if (tempstr.Length > 14)
                {
                    if (mo.Properties_.Item(Name).CIMType ==
WbemCimtypeEnum.wbemCimtypeDatetime)
                    {
```

```
                    return tempstr.Substring(5, 2) + "/" +
tempstr.Substring(7, 2) + "/" + tempstr.Substring(0, 4) + " " +
tempstr.Substring(9, 2) + ":" + tempstr.Substring(11, 2) + ":" +
tempstr.Substring(13, 2);
                }
            }
            return tempstr;
        }
        else
        {
            return "";
        }
    }

}
}
```

To show you how much more you get from ___InstanceModificationEvent, here's the results from just 29 of them: (Which took all of 5 seconds)

Caption	CommandLine
System Idle Process	
dwm.exe	\dwm.exe\
svchost.exe	C:\\Windows\\System32\\svchost.exe -k netsvcs
nvcontainer.exe	\C:\\Program Files\\NVIDIA Corporation\\NvContainer\\nvcontainer.exe\ -s NvContainerLocalSystem -a -f C:\\ProgramData\\NVI
MsMpEng.exe	
IntelliTrace.exe	\C:\\Program Files (x86)\\Microsoft Visual Studio 10.0\\Team Tools\\TraceDebugger Tools\\IntelliTrace.exe\ run /name:wpfapplicat
explorer.exe	C:\\Windows\\Explorer.EXE
NVIDIA Web Helper.exe	\C:\\Program Files (x86)\\NVIDIA Corporation\\NvNode\\NVIDIA Web Helper.exe\ index.js
WmiPrvSE.exe	C:\\Windows\\system32\\wbem\\wmiprvse.exe
NisSrv.exe	
WpfApplication6.vshost.exe	\c:\\users\\administrator\\documents\\visual studio 2010\\Projects\\WpfApplication6\\WpfApplication6\\bin\\Debug\\WpfApplic
firefox.exe	\C:\\Program Files (x86)\\Mozilla Firefox\\firefox.exe\ -contentproc --channel=\6688.20.2080931576\\1509301771\ -childID 3 -isF
csrss.exe	
MpCmdRun.exe	\C:\\ProgramData\\Microsoft\\Windows Defender\\Platform\\4.18.1807.18075-0\\MpCmdRun.exe\ SpyNetServiceDss -RestrictPri
firefox.exe	\C:\\Program Files (x86)\\Mozilla Firefox\\firefox.exe\
devenv.exe	\C:\\Program Files (x86)\\Microsoft Visual Studio 10.0\\Common7\\IDE\\devenv.exe\
System Idle Process	
svchost.exe	C:\\Windows\\System32\\svchost.exe -k netsvcs
NvTelemetryContainer.exe	\C:\\Program Files (x86)\\NVIDIA Corporation\\NvTelemetry\\NvTelemetryContainer.exe\ -s NvTelemetryContainer -f C:\\Program
nvcontainer.exe	\C:\\Program Files\\NVIDIA Corporation\\NvContainer\\nvcontainer.exe\ -s NvContainerLocalSystem -a -f C:\\ProgramData\\NVI
MsMpEng.exe	
IntelliTrace.exe	\C:\\Program Files (x86)\\Microsoft Visual Studio 10.0\\Team Tools\\TraceDebugger Tools\\IntelliTrace.exe\ run /name:wpfapplicat
NVIDIA Web Helper.exe	\C:\\Program Files (x86)\\NVIDIA Corporation\\NvNode\\NVIDIA Web Helper.exe\ index.js
firefox.exe	\C:\\Program Files (x86)\\Mozilla Firefox\\firefox.exe\ -contentproc --channel=\6688.3.1907855476\\931673671\ -childID 1 -isFor
WmiPrvSE.exe	C:\\Windows\\system32\\wbem\\wmiprvse.exe
WpfApplication6.vshost.exe	\c:\\users\\administrator\\documents\\visual studio 2010\\Projects\\WpfApplication6\\WpfApplication6\\bin\\Debug\\WpfApplic
firefox.exe	\C:\\Program Files (x86)\\Mozilla Firefox\\firefox.exe\ -contentproc --channel=\6688.20.2080931576\\1509301771\ -childID 3 -isF
csrss.exe	
unsecapp.exe	C:\\Windows\\system32\\wbem\\unsecapp.exe -Embedding
firefox.exe	\C:\\Program Files (x86)\\Mozilla Firefox\\firefox.exe\
devenv.exe	\C:\\Program Files (x86)\\Microsoft Visual Studio 10.0\\Common7\\IDE\\devenv.exe\
svchost.exe	C:\\Windows\\System32\\svchost.exe -k LocalServiceNetworkRestricted

Code for __InstanceOperationEvent:

Here's the MainWindow.xaml.cs code for InstanceOperationEvent.

```csharp
using System;
using System.Collections.Generic;
using System.Linq;
using System.Text;
using System.Windows;
using System.Windows.Controls;
using System.Windows.Data;
using System.Windows.Documents;
using System.Windows.Input;
using System.Windows.Media;
using System.Windows.Media.Imaging;
using System.Windows.Shapes;
using System.Data;
using System.Collections.ObjectModel;
using Scripting;
using WbemScripting;

namespace WpfApplication12
{
    /// <summary>
    /// Interaction logic for Window2.xaml
    /// </summary>
    ///
    public partial class MainWindow : Window
    {
        public MainWindow()
        {
            InitializeComponent();

        }

        Form4 myform = null;
        private void Window_Loaded(object sender, RoutedEventArgs e)
        {
            myform = new Form4();
            myform.Visible = false;
            myform.Start_Async_Code();
```

```
            System.Data.DataTable dt = myform.dt;
            GridView gv = new GridView();
            Binding bi = null;
            DataGridTextColumn c = null;



            foreach (System.Data.DataColumn column in dt.Columns)
            {

                bi = new Binding(column.Caption);
                c = new DataGridTextColumn();
                c.Header = column.Caption;
                c.Binding = bi;
                dataGrid1.Columns.Add(c);
            }

            this.dataGrid1.DataContext = dt;
        }

    }
}
```

Here's the form's code:

```
using System;
using System.Collections.Generic;
using System.ComponentModel;
using System.Data;
using System.Drawing;
using System.Linq;
using System.Text;
using System.Windows.Forms;
using Scripting;
using WbemScripting;

namespace WpfApplication12
{
    public partial class Form4 : Form
```

```csharp
{
    public Form4()
    {
        InitializeComponent();
    }
    SWbemSink sink = null;
    public System.Data.DataTable dt = new
System.Data.DataTable();
    int v = 0;
    int w = 0;
    private void sink_OnCompleted(WbemScripting.WbemErrorEnum
iHResult, WbemScripting.SWbemObject objWbemErrorObject,
WbemScripting.SWbemNamedValueSet objWbemAsyncContext)
    {
        w = 1;
    }
    public void sink_OnObjectReady(WbemScripting.SWbemObject
objWbemObject, WbemScripting.SWbemNamedValueSet
objWbemAsyncContext)
    {

        SWbemObject obj =
objWbemObject.Properties_.Item("TargetInstance").get_Value();

        if (v == 0)
        {
            dt.Columns.Add("Event Type");
            foreach (SWbemProperty prop in obj.Properties_)
            {
                dt.Columns.Add(prop.Name);
            }
            v = 1;
        }

        switch (objWbemObject.Path_.Class)
        {

            case "__InstanceCreationEvent":

                System.Data.DataRow dr = dt.NewRow();
                dr["Event Type"] = "__InstanceCreationEvent";

                foreach (SWbemProperty prop in
obj.Properties_)
                {
```

```
                    dr[prop.Name] =
GetManagementValue(prop.Name, obj);
                    }
                    dt.Rows.Add(dr);

                    v = v + 1;
                    if(v == 6)
                    {
                        sink.Cancel();
                    }
                    break;

            case "__InstanceDeletionEvent":

                    dr = dt.NewRow();
                    dr["Event Type"] = "__InstanceDeletionEvent";

                    foreach (SWbemProperty prop in
obj.Properties_)
                    {
                        dr[prop.Name] =
GetManagementValue(prop.Name, obj);
                    }
                    dt.Rows.Add(dr);

                    v = v + 1;
                    if(v == 6)
                    {
                        sink.Cancel();
                    }
                    break;

            case "__InstanceModificationEvent":

                    dr = dt.NewRow();
                    dr["Event Type"] =
"__InstanceModificationEvent";

                    foreach (SWbemProperty prop in
obj.Properties_)
                    {
                        dr[prop.Name] =
GetManagementValue(prop.Name, obj);
                    }
                    dt.Rows.Add(dr);
```

```
                    v = v + 1;
                    if(v == 6)
                    {
                        sink.Cancel();
                    }


                    break;

                }


        }
        public void Start_Async_Code()
        {

            SWbemLocator l = new SWbemLocator();
            SWbemServices svc = l.ConnectServer("LocalHost",
"root\\cimv2", "", "", "MS_409", "", 128, null);
            svc.Security_.AuthenticationLevel =
WbemAuthenticationLevelEnum.wbemAuthenticationLevelPktPrivacy;
            svc.Security_.ImpersonationLevel =
WbemImpersonationLevelEnum.wbemImpersonationLevelImpersonate;
            sink = new SWbemSink();
            sink.OnCompleted += new
ISWbemSinkEvents_OnCompletedEventHandler(sink_OnCompleted);
            sink.OnObjectReady += new
ISWbemSinkEvents_OnObjectReadyEventHandler(sink_OnObjectReady);

            svc.ExecNotificationQueryAsync(sink, "Select * From
__InstanceOperationEvent within 1 where TargetInstance ISA
'Win32_Process'");
            while (w == 0)
            {
                System.Windows.Forms.Application.DoEvents();
            }

        }
        private System.String GetManagementValue(System.String
Name, SWbemObject mo)
        {
            int pos = 0;
            System.String tName = Name + " = ";
            System.String tempstr = mo.GetObjectText_(0);
```

```
            pos = tempstr.IndexOf(tName);
            if (pos > -1)
            {
                pos = pos + tName.Length;
                tempstr = tempstr.Substring(pos, tempstr.Length -
pos);

                pos = tempstr.IndexOf(";");
                tempstr = tempstr.Substring(0, pos);
                tempstr = tempstr.Replace("\"", "");
                tempstr = tempstr.Replace("{", "");
                tempstr = tempstr.Replace("}", "");
                if (tempstr.Length > 14)
                {
                    if (mo.Properties_.Item(Name).CIMType ==
WbemCimtypeEnum.wbemCimtypeDatetime)
                    {
                        return tempstr.Substring(5, 2) + "/" +
tempstr.Substring(7, 2) + "/" + tempstr.Substring(0, 4) + " " +
tempstr.Substring(9, 2) + ":" + tempstr.Substring(11, 2) + ":" +
tempstr.Substring(13, 2);
                    }
                }
                return tempstr;
            }
            else
            {
                return "";
            }
        }

    }
}
```

Notice that I did something a bit differently here. I added the EventClass property to the table. It is the only way to know what class was responsible for the event.

The select case statement is currently set to use all three. But you can either do all three or a combination of 1, 2 or all three.

Below is the results using just Creation and deletion as I wasn't fast enough to create and delete the calculator before the darn thing filled up with ModificationEvents.

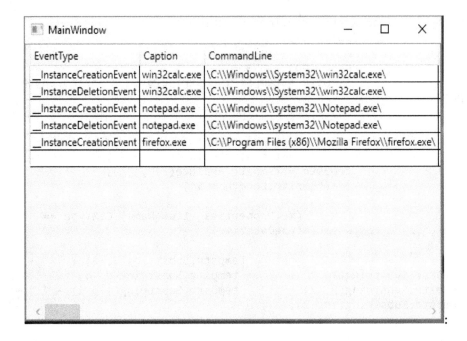

So, there you have it. WPF using a DataGridView with WMI in Async mode using a Horizontal View.

GET ASYNC IN VERTICAL FORMAT

The rows become columns and the columns become rows. That sounds simple enough, right?

So, here's the code for GetAsync:

```csharp
using System;
using System.Collections.Generic;
using System.ComponentModel;
using System.Data;
using System.Drawing;
using System.Linq;
using System.Text;
using System.Windows.Forms;
using Scripting;
using WbemScripting;

namespace WpfApplication12
{
    public partial class Form1 : Form
    {
        public Form1()
        {
            InitializeComponent();
        }
        SWbemSink sink = null;
        public System.Data.DataTable dt = new
System.Data.DataTable();
        int v = 0;
        int w = 0;
```

```csharp
        int x = 0;
        int y = 0;

        private void sink_OnCompleted(WbemScripting.WbemErrorEnum
iHResult, WbemScripting.SWbemObject objWbemErrorObject,
WbemScripting.SWbemNamedValueSet objWbemAsyncContext)
        {


        }
        public void sink_OnObjectReady(WbemScripting.SWbemObject
objWbemObject, WbemScripting.SWbemNamedValueSet
objWbemAsyncContext)
        {

            if (v == 0)
            {
                dt.Columns.Add("Property Name");
                foreach (SWbemProperty prop in
objWbemObject.Properties_)
                {
                    System.Data.DataRow dr = dt.NewRow();
                    dr["Property Name"] = prop.Name;
                    dt.Rows.Add(dr);
                }
                V=1;
            }
            SWbemObjectSet objs = objWbemObject.Instances_(0,
null);

            foreach (SWbemObject obj in objs)
            {
                dt.Columns.Add("Row" + y);
                foreach (SWbemProperty prop in obj.Properties_)
                {
                    dt.Rows[x]["Row" + y] =
GetManagementValue(prop.Name, obj);
                    x=x+1;
                }
                x=0;
                y=y+1;
            }
            w = 1;
        }
        public void Start_Async_Code()
```

```csharp
        {
            SWbemLocator l = new SWbemLocator();
            SWbemServices svc = l.ConnectServer("LocalHost",
"root\\cimv2", "", "", "MS_409", "", 128, null);
            svc.Security_.AuthenticationLevel =
WbemAuthenticationLevelEnum.wbemAuthenticationLevelPktPrivacy;
            svc.Security_.ImpersonationLevel =
WbemImpersonationLevelEnum.wbemImpersonationLevelImpersonate;
            sink = new SWbemSink();
            sink.OnCompleted += new
ISWbemSinkEvents_OnCompletedEventHandler(sink_OnCompleted);
            sink.OnObjectReady += new
ISWbemSinkEvents_OnObjectReadyEventHandler(sink_OnObjectReady);
            svc.GetAsync(sink, "Win32_BIOS");

            while (w == 0)
            {
                System.Windows.Forms.Application.DoEvents();
            }

        }
        private System.String GetManagementValue(System.String
Name, SWbemObject mo)
        {
            int pos = 0;
            System.String tName = Name + " = ";
            System.String tempstr = mo.GetObjectText_(0);
            pos = tempstr.IndexOf(tName);
            if (pos > -1)
            {
                pos = pos + tName.Length;
                tempstr = tempstr.Substring(pos, tempstr.Length -
pos);
                pos = tempstr.IndexOf(";");
                tempstr = tempstr.Substring(0, pos);
                tempstr = tempstr.Replace("\"", "");
                tempstr = tempstr.Replace("{", "");
                tempstr = tempstr.Replace("}", "");
                if (tempstr.Length > 14)
                {
                    if (mo.Properties_.Item(Name).CIMType ==
WbemCimtypeEnum.wbemCimtypeDatetime)
                    {
```

```
                    return tempstr.Substring(5, 2) + "/" +
tempstr.Substring(7, 2) + "/" + tempstr.Substring(0, 4) + " " +
tempstr.Substring(9, 2) + ":" + tempstr.Substring(11, 2) + ":" +
tempstr.Substring(13, 2);
                    }
                }
                return tempstr;
            }
            else
            {
                return "";
            }
        }

    }

}
```

Output:

Property Name	Row0
BiosCharacteristics	7, 11, 12, 15, 16, 17, 19, 23, 24, 25, 26, 27, 28, 29, 32, 33, 40, 42, 43
BIOSVersion	ALASKA - 1072009, BIOS Date: 04/15/16 08:59:39 Ver: 04.06.05, BIOS Date: 04/15/16 08:59:39 Ver: 04.06.05
BuildNumber	
Caption	BIOS Date: 04/15/16 08:59:39 Ver: 04.06.05
CodeSet	
CurrentLanguage	en|US|iso8859-1
Description	BIOS Date: 04/15/16 08:59:39 Ver: 04.06.05
EmbeddedControllerMajorVersion	255
EmbeddedControllerMinorVersion	255
IdentificationCode	
InstallableLanguages	8
InstallDate	
LanguageEdition	
ListOfLanguages	en|US|iso8859-1, fr|FR|iso8859-1, es|ES|iso8859-1, de|DE|iso8859-1, ru|RU|iso8859-5, ja|P|unicode, zh|TW|unicode, zh|CN|unicode
Manufacturer	American Megatrends Inc.
Name	BIOS Date: 04/15/16 08:59:39 Ver: 04.06.05
OtherTargetOS	
PrimaryBIOS	TRUE
ReleaseDate	41/50/2016 00:00:0.
SerialNumber	To be filled by O.E.M.
SMBIOSBIOSVersion	0901
SMBIOSMajorVersion	2
SMBIOSMinorVersion	7
SMBIOSPresent	TRUE
SoftwareElementID	BIOS Date: 04/15/16 08:59:39 Ver: 04.06.05
SoftwareElementState	3
Status	OK
SystemBiosMajorVersion	4
SystemBiosMinorVersion	6
TargetOperatingSystem	0
Version	ALASKA - 1072009, BIOS Date: 04/15/16 08:59:39 Ver: 04.06.05, BIOS Date: 04/15/16 08:59:39 Ver: 04.06.05

Of Course, Win32_BIOS only returns a single row of data. Let's switch the Win32_BIOS class to something that will return more than one row:

The results:

Property Name	Row0	Row1
Caption	System Idle Process	System
CommandLine		
CreationClassName	Win32_Process	Win32_Process
CreationDate	82/92/2018 32:90:9.	82/92/2018 32:90:9.
CSCreationClassName	Win32_ComputerSystem	Win32_ComputerSystem
CSName	WIN-QM2FHP9BMJG	WIN-QM2FHP9BMJG
Description	System Idle Process	System
ExecutablePath		
ExecutionState		
Handle	0	4
HandleCount	0	1173
InstallDate		
KernelModeTime	11170901562500	18216406250
MaximumWorkingSetSize		
MinimumWorkingSetSize		
Name	Win32_Process	Win32_Process
OSCreationClassName	Win32_OperatingSystem	Win32_OperatingSystem
OSName	Microsoft Windows Server 2016 Datacenter Ev.	Microsoft Windows Server 2016 Datacenter Evaluation|C:\\Wind
OtherOperationCount	0	12202
OtherTransferCount	0	422230
PageFaults	2	4299
PageFileUsage	0	128
ParentProcessId	0	0
PeakPageFileUsage	0	140
PeakVirtualSize	65536	11358208

INSTANCESOF ASYNC IN VERTICAL FORMAT

The rows become columns and the columns become rows. That sounds simple enough, right? So, here's the code for InstancesOfAsync:

```csharp
using System;
using System.Collections.Generic;
using System.ComponentModel;
using System.Data;
using System.Drawing;
using System.Linq;
using System.Text;
using System.Windows.Forms;
using Scripting;
using WbemScripting;

namespace WpfApplication12
{
    public partial class Form6 : Form
    {
        public Form6()
        {
            InitializeComponent();
        }
        SWbemSink sink = null;
        public System.Data.DataTable dt = new
System.Data.DataTable();

        int v = 0;
```

```csharp
        int w = 0;
        int x = 0;
        int y = 0;


        private void sink_OnCompleted(WbemScripting.WbemErrorEnum
iHResult, WbemScripting.SWbemObject objWbemErrorObject,
WbemScripting.SWbemNamedValueSet objWbemAsyncContext)
        {

            w = 1;

        }
        public void sink_OnObjectReady(WbemScripting.SWbemObject
objWbemObject, WbemScripting.SWbemNamedValueSet
objWbemAsyncContext)
        {

            if (v == 0)
            {
                dt.Columns.Add("Property Name");
                foreach (SWbemProperty prop in
objWbemObject.Properties_)
                {
                    System.Data.DataRow dr = dt.NewRow();
                    dr["Property Name"] = prop.Name;
                    dt.Rows.Add(dr);
                }
                v=1;
            }

            dt.Columns.Add("Row" + y);
            foreach (SWbemProperty prop in
objWbemObject.Properties_)
            {
                dt.Rows[x]["Row" + y] =
GetManagementValue(prop.Name, objWbemObject);
                x=x+1;
            }
            x=0;
            y=y+1;
        }
        public void Start_Async_Code()
        {

            SWbemLocator l = new SWbemLocator();
```

```csharp
            SWbemServices svc = l.ConnectServer("LocalHost",
"root\\cimv2", "", "", "MS_409", "", 128, null);
            svc.Security_.AuthenticationLevel =
WbemAuthenticationLevelEnum.wbemAuthenticationLevelPktPrivacy;
            svc.Security_.ImpersonationLevel =
WbemImpersonationLevelEnum.wbemImpersonationLevelImpersonate;
            sink = new SWbemSink();
            sink.OnCompleted += new
ISWbemSinkEvents_OnCompletedEventHandler(sink_OnCompleted);
            sink.OnObjectReady += new
ISWbemSinkEvents_OnObjectReadyEventHandler(sink_OnObjectReady);
            svc.InstancesOfAsync(sink,
"Win32_NetWorkLoginProfile");

            while (w == 0)
            {
                System.Windows.Forms.Application.DoEvents();
            }

        }
        private System.String GetManagementValue(System.String
Name, SWbemObject mo)
        {
            int pos = 0;
            System.String tName = Name + " = ";
            System.String tempstr = mo.GetObjectText_(0);
            pos = tempstr.IndexOf(tName);
            if (pos > -1)
            {
                pos = pos + tName.Length;
                tempstr = tempstr.Substring(pos, tempstr.Length -
pos);
                pos = tempstr.IndexOf(";");
                tempstr = tempstr.Substring(0, pos);
                tempstr = tempstr.Replace("\"", "");
                tempstr = tempstr.Replace("{", "");
                tempstr = tempstr.Replace("}", "");
                if (tempstr.Length > 14)
                {
                    if (mo.Properties_.Item(Name).CIMType ==
WbemCimtypeEnum.wbemCimtypeDatetime)
                    {
                        return tempstr.Substring(5, 2) + "/" +
tempstr.Substring(7, 2) + "/" + tempstr.Substring(0, 4) + " " +
```

```
tempstr.Substring(9, 2) + ":" + tempstr.Substring(11, 2) + ":" +
tempstr.Substring(13, 2);
                    }
                }
                return tempstr;
            }
            else
            {
                return "";
            }
        }

    }

}
```

Output:

Property Name	Row0	Row1
AccountExpires		
AuthorizationFlags		
BadPasswordCount		
Caption	NT AUTHORITY\\SYSTEM	NT AUTHORITY\\LOCAL SERVICE
CodePage		
Comment		
CountryCode		
Description	Network login profile settings for SYS1	Network login profile settings for LOCAL SERVICE on
Flags		
FullName		
HomeDirectory		
HomeDirectoryDrive		
LastLogoff		
LastLogon		

MainWindow

EXECQUERY ASYNC IN VERTICAL FORMAT

T he rows become columns and the columns become rows. That sounds simple enough, right? So, here's the code for ExecQueryAsync:

```csharp
using System;
using System.Collections.Generic;
using System.ComponentModel;
using System.Data;
using System.Drawing;
using System.Linq;
using System.Text;
using System.Windows.Forms;
using Scripting;
using WbemScripting;

namespace WpfApplication12
{
    public partial class Form6 : Form
    {
        public Form6()
        {
            InitializeComponent();
        }
```

```csharp
        SWbemSink sink = null;
        public System.Data.DataTable dt = new
System.Data.DataTable();

        int v = 0;
        int w = 0;
        int x = 0;
        int y = 0;

        private void sink_OnCompleted(WbemScripting.WbemErrorEnum
iHResult, WbemScripting.SWbemObject objWbemErrorObject,
WbemScripting.SWbemNamedValueSet objWbemAsyncContext)
        {

            w = 1;

        }
        public void sink_OnObjectReady(WbemScripting.SWbemObject
objWbemObject, WbemScripting.SWbemNamedValueSet
objWbemAsyncContext)
        {

        if (v == 0)
        {
            dt.Columns.Add("Property Name");
            foreach (SWbemProperty prop in
objWbemObject.Properties_)
                {
                    System.Data.DataRow dr = dt.NewRow();
                    dr["Property Name"] = prop.Name;
                    dt.Rows.Add(dr);
                }
                v=1;
        }

        dt.Columns.Add("Row" + y);
        foreach (SWbemProperty prop in
objWbemObject.Properties_)
        {
            dt.Rows[x]["Row" + y] =
GetManagementValue(prop.Name, objWbemObject);
            x=x+1;
        }
        x=0;
        y=y+1;
```

```
        }
        public void Start_Async_Code()
        {

            SWbemLocator l = new SWbemLocator();
            SWbemServices svc = l.ConnectServer("LocalHost",
"root\\cimv2", "", "", "MS_409", "", 128, null);
            svc.Security_.AuthenticationLevel =
WbemAuthenticationLevelEnum.wbemAuthenticationLevelPktPrivacy;
            svc.Security_.ImpersonationLevel =
WbemImpersonationLevelEnum.wbemImpersonationLevelImpersonate;
            sink = new SWbemSink();
            sink.OnCompleted += new
ISWbemSinkEvents_OnCompletedEventHandler(sink_OnCompleted);
            sink.OnObjectReady += new
ISWbemSinkEvents_OnObjectReadyEventHandler(sink_OnObjectReady);
            svc.ExecQueryAsync(sink,
"Win32_NetWorkLoginProfile");

            while (w == 0)
            {
                System.Windows.Forms.Application.DoEvents();
            }

        }
        private System.String GetManagementValue(System.String
Name, SWbemObject mo)
        {
            int pos = 0;
            System.String tName = Name + " = ";
            System.String tempstr = mo.GetObjectText_(0);
            pos = tempstr.IndexOf(tName);
            if (pos > -1)
            {
                pos = pos + tName.Length;
                tempstr = tempstr.Substring(pos, tempstr.Length -
pos);
                pos = tempstr.IndexOf(";");
                tempstr = tempstr.Substring(0, pos);
                tempstr = tempstr.Replace("\"", "");
                tempstr = tempstr.Replace("{", "");
                tempstr = tempstr.Replace("}", "");
                if (tempstr.Length > 14)
                {
```

```
                if (mo.Properties_.Item(Name).CIMType ==
WbemCimtypeEnum.wbemCimtypeDatetime)
                    {
                        return tempstr.Substring(5, 2) + "/" +
tempstr.Substring(7, 2) + "/" + tempstr.Substring(0, 4) + " " +
tempstr.Substring(9, 2) + ":" + tempstr.Substring(11, 2) + ":" +
tempstr.Substring(13, 2);
                    }
                }
                return tempstr;
            }
            else
            {
                return "";
            }
        }

    }

}
```

Output:

Property Name	Row0	Row1
AccountExpires		
AuthorizationFlags		
BadPasswordCount		
Caption	NT AUTHORITY\\SYSTEM	NT AUTHORITY\\LOCAL SERVICE
CodePage		
Comment		
CountryCode		
Description	Network login profile settings for SYS1	Network login profile settings for LOCAL SERVICE on
Flags		
FullName		
HomeDirectory		
HomeDirectoryDrive		
LastLogoff		
LastLogon		

MainWindow — □ ×

EXECNOTIFICATIONQUERY ASYNC IN VERTICAL FORMAT

T he rows become columns and the columns become rows. That sounds simple enough, right? So, here's the code for ExecNotificationQueryAsync:

```csharp
using System;
using System.Collections.Generic;
using System.ComponentModel;
using System.Data;
using System.Drawing;
using System.Linq;
using System.Text;
using System.Windows.Forms;
using Scripting;
using WbemScripting;

namespace WpfApplication12
{
    public partial class Form7 : Form
    {
        public Form7()
        {
            InitializeComponent();
        }
```

```csharp
        SWbemSink sink = null;
        public System.Data.DataTable dt = new
System.Data.DataTable();

        int v = 0;
        int w = 0;
        int x = 0;
        int y = 0;

        private void sink_OnCompleted(WbemScripting.WbemErrorEnum
iHResult, WbemScripting.SWbemObject objWbemErrorObject,
WbemScripting.SWbemNamedValueSet objWbemAsyncContext)
        {

            w = 1;

        }
        public void sink_OnObjectReady(WbemScripting.SWbemObject
objWbemObject, WbemScripting.SWbemNamedValueSet
objWbemAsyncContext)
        {

            SWbemObject obj =
objWbemObject.Properties_.Item("TargetInstance").get_Value();
            if (v == 0)
            {

                dt.Columns.Add("Property Name");

                System.Data.DataRow dr = dt.NewRow();
                dr["Property Name"] = "Event Type";
                dt.Rows.Add(dr);

                foreach (SWbemProperty prop in obj.Properties_)
                {
                    dr = dt.NewRow();
                    dr["Property Name"] = prop.Name;
                    dt.Rows.Add(dr);
                }
                v = 1;
            }


            if (objWbemObject.Path_.Class !=
"__InstanceModificationEvent")
```

```
                {
                    dt.Columns.Add("Row" + y);
                    dt.Rows[x]["Row" + y] =
objWbemObject.Path_.Class;
                    foreach (SWbemProperty prop in obj.Properties_)
                    {
                        dt.Rows[x + 1]["Row" + y] =
GetManagementValue(prop.Name, obj);
                        x = x + 1;
                    }
                    x = 0;
                    if (y == 7)
                    {
                        sink.Cancel();
                    }
                    y = y + 1;
                }


        }
        public void Start_Async_Code()
        {

            SWbemLocator l = new SWbemLocator();
            SWbemServices svc = l.ConnectServer("LocalHost",
"root\\cimv2", "", "", "MS_409", "", 128, null);
            svc.Security_.AuthenticationLevel =
WbemAuthenticationLevelEnum.wbemAuthenticationLevelPktPrivacy;
            svc.Security_.ImpersonationLevel =
WbemImpersonationLevelEnum.wbemImpersonationLevelImpersonate;
            sink = new SWbemSink();
            sink.OnCompleted += new
ISWbemSinkEvents_OnCompletedEventHandler(sink_OnCompleted);
            sink.OnObjectReady += new
ISWbemSinkEvents_OnObjectReadyEventHandler(sink_OnObjectReady);
            svc.ExecNotificationQueryAsync(sink, "Select * from
__InstanceOperationEvent within 1 where TargetInstance ISA
'Win32_Process'");

            while (w == 0)
            {
                System.Windows.Forms.Application.DoEvents();
            }

        }
```

```
        private System.String GetManagementValue(System.String
Name, SWbemObject mo)
        {
            int pos = 0;
            System.String tName = Name + " = ";
            System.String tempstr = mo.GetObjectText_(0);
            pos = tempstr.IndexOf(tName);
            if (pos > -1)
            {
                pos = pos + tName.Length;
                tempstr = tempstr.Substring(pos, tempstr.Length -
pos);
                pos = tempstr.IndexOf(";");
                tempstr = tempstr.Substring(0, pos);
                tempstr = tempstr.Replace("\"", "");
                tempstr = tempstr.Replace("{", "");
                tempstr = tempstr.Replace("}", "");
                if (tempstr.Length > 14)
                {
                    if (mo.Properties_.Item(Name).CIMType ==
WbemCimtypeEnum.wbemCimtypeDatetime)
                    {
                        return tempstr.Substring(5, 2) + "/" +
tempstr.Substring(7, 2) + "/" + tempstr.Substring(0, 4) + " " +
tempstr.Substring(9, 2) + ":" + tempstr.Substring(11, 2) + ":" +
tempstr.Substring(13, 2);
                    }
                }
                return tempstr;
            }
            else
            {
                return "";
            }
        }

    }

}
```

Output:

For ___InstanceCreationEvent:

Property Name	Row0
Event Type	_InstanceCreationEvent
Caption	MSACCESS.EXE
CommandLine	\C:\\Program Files (x86)\\Microsoft Office\\root\\Office16\\MSA(
CreationClassName	Win32_Process
CreationDate	83/11/2018 92:25:8.
CSCreationClassName	Win32_ComputerSystem
CSName	WIN-QM2FHP9BMJG
Description	MSACCESS.EXE
ExecutablePath	C:\\Program Files (x86)\\Microsoft Office\\root\\Office16\\MSAC
ExecutionState	
Handle	4040
HandleCount	197
InstallDate	
KernelModeTime	2656250

For ___InstanceDeletionEvent:

Property Name	Row0
Event Type	_InstanceDeletionEvent
Caption	firefox.exe
CommandLine	\C:\\Program Files (x86)\\Mozilla Firefox\\firefox.exe\ -contentpr
CreationClassName	Win32_Process
CreationDate	83/11/2018 92:71:0.
CSCreationClassName	Win32_ComputerSystem
CSName	WIN-QM2FHP9BMJG
Description	firefox.exe
ExecutablePath	C:\\Program Files (x86)\\Mozilla Firefox\\firefox.exe
ExecutionState	
Handle	4800
HandleCount	408
InstallDate	
KernelModeTime	3906250

I neutered ___InstanceModificationEvent because I'm too darn slow to show all three in action.

Anyway, we've covered a lot of territory with this book. Good luck!

www.ingramcontent.com/pod-product-compliance
Lightning Source LLC
Chambersburg PA
CBHW070853070326
40690CB00009B/1820